A TASTE OF
CHICKEN SOUP
FOR THE
GRANDPARENT'S SOUL

**Stories to Open the Hearts and
Rekindle the Spirits of
Grandparents**

Jack Canfield
Mark Victor Hansen
Meladee McCarty
Hanoch McCarty

Health Communications, Inc.
Deerfield Beach, Florida

www.hcibooks.com
www.chickensoup.com

The Antique. Reprinted by permission of Harriet May Savitz. ©2000 Harriet May Savitz.

Computer Granny. Reprinted by permission of Kay Conner Pliszka. ©1996 Kay Conner Pliszka.

A Doll of a Christmas. Reprinted by permission of Cookie Curci. ©1995 Cookie Curci.

The Smooth Stone. Reprinted by permission of Walker W. Meade. ©1999 Walker W. Meade.

Passing the Torch. Reprinted by permission of Marnie O. Mamminga. ©1994 Marnie O. Mamminga.

Worms and All. Reprinted by permission of Pamela Jenkins. ©2000 Pamela Jenkins.

What's a Grandma to Do? Reprinted by permission of Patricia Lorenz. ©1999 Patricia Lorenz.

She'll Call Me "Ma." Reprinted by permission of Jackie Davis. ©1999 Jackie Davis.

Mrs. Malaprop's Kin. Reprinted by permission of Sharon Landeen. ©2001 Sharon Landeen.

Gramma, Please Don't Make Me Put Them Back! Reprinted by permission of Karren E. Key. ©2000 Karren E. Key.

The Marriage License. Reprinted by permission of Meladee McCarty ©1999 Meladee McCarty.

The Rodeo Grandmas. Reprinted by permission of Hanoch McCarty ©2001 Hanoch McCarty.

**Library of Congress Cataloging-in-Publication Data
is available form the Library of Congress.**

© 2005 Jack Canfield and Mark Victor Hansen
ISBN 0-7573-0436-2

Publisher: Health Communications Inc.,
        3201 SW 15th Street, Deerfield Beach, FL 33442

To Rand Avery Hinds, Hanoch and Meladee's
beautiful four-year-old granddaughter,
and all the other beautiful grandchildren
yet to arrive in our families whose names
we do not know. Our love for each of you
has been reserved in a special place in our hearts.

Contents

Introduction

Grandparents are alive and well in America. They are allies for grandchildren and have the time to really pay attention to little ones' concerns. They provide child care that enables their sons and daughters to work to support their growing families.

Grandparents are the axles of the wheel of the family. There are many kinds of grandmas and grandpas, from the kind we read about in stories with Norman Rockwell illustrations to incredibly active grandparents, flying all over, doing jobs they'd never consider retiring from, conquering the Internet and e-mail, and performing essential, irreplaceable services for their communities.

Grandparents are living longer, doing more and refusing to accept any limitations. But they still make a difference, one at a time, for their grandchildren. In our highly mobile society, they may live far from their grandkids, but they so often serve as the anchor, the steadying point that helps give meaning and safety to those children's lives. Some grandparents are courageously parenting their grandchildren — and we celebrate them.

Join us in celebrating grandparenthood through the power of these stories we have excerpted from the bestseller, *Chicken Soup for the Grandparent's Soul*, published in 2002.

Read them; savor them, one at a time. Read them aloud to family and others you love. And then pause and tell your own stories, one at a time.

It is remarkable how, overnight,
a quiet mature lady can learn
to sit cross-legged on the floor
and play a tin drum, quack like
a duck, sing all the verses of
"The Twelve Days of Christmas,"
make paper flowers, draw pigs
and sew on the ears of severely-
injured teddy bears.

Marlene Walkington Ferber

The Antique

Love doesn't make the world go 'round. Love is what makes the ride worthwhile.

Franklin P. Jones

My six-year-old granddaughter stares at me as if she is seeing me for the first time. "Grandma, you are an antique," she says. "You are old. Antiques are old. You are my antique."

I am not satisfied to let the matter rest there. I take out *Webster's Dictionary* and read the definition to Jenny. I explain, "An antique is not only just old; it's an object existing since or belonging to earlier times . . . a work of art . . . a piece of furniture.

Antiques are treasured," I tell Jenny as I put away the dictionary. "They have to be handled carefully because they sometimes are very valuable."

According to various customs laws, in order to be qualified as an antique, the object has to be at least one hundred years old.

"I'm only sixty-seven," I remind Jenny.

We look around the house for other antiques besides me. There is a bureau that was handed down from one aunt to another and finally to our family. "It's very old," I tell Jenny. "I try to keep it polished, and I show it off whenever I can. You do that with antiques." When Jenny gets older and understands such things, I might also tell her that whenever I look at the bureau or touch it, I am reminded of the aunt so dear to me who gave me the bureau as a gift. I see her face again, though she is no longer with us. I even hear her voice and recall her smile. I remember myself as a little girl leaning against this antique, listening to one of her stories. The bureau does that for me.

There is a picture on the wall purchased

at a garage sale. It is dated 1867. "Now that's an antique," I boast. "Over one hundred years old." Of course it is marked up and scratched and not in very good condition. "Sometimes age does that," I tell Jenny. "But the marks are good marks. They show living, being around. That's something to display with pride. In fact, sometimes, the more an object shows age, the more valuable it can become." It is important that I believe this for my own self-esteem.

Our tour of antiques continues. There is a vase on the floor. It has been in my household for a long time. I'm not certain where it came from, but I didn't buy it new. And then there is the four-poster bed, sent to me forty years ago from an uncle who slept in it for fifty years.

The one thing about antiques, I explain to Jenny, is that they usually have a story. They've been in one home and then another, handed down from one family to another, traveling all over the place. They've lasted through years and years. They could have been tossed away, or ignored, or destroyed or lost. But instead, they survived.

For a moment Jenny looks thoughtful. "I

don't have any antiques but you," she says. Then her face brightens. "Could I take you to school for show-and-tell?"

"Only if I fit into your backpack," I answer.

And then her antique lifted her up and embraced her in a hug that would last through the years.

Harriet May Savitz

Computer Granny

Other things may change us, but we start and end with family.

Anthony Brandt

My eyes filled with tears as I kissed my family good-bye at the Sydney, Australia, airport. Because the trip from America is so expensive, I knew I wouldn't be returning to be with my son, my Australian daughter-in-law or my precious grandchildren for at least two more years.

Tracy, nine years old, and Phillip, eleven, were born there. I'd seen them only five times in their short lives-one month every two years. I so wanted to be a good grandma to them, like my grandma was to me. I wanted to bake them homemade cookies, visit their schools, watch Tracy's dance recitals and Phillip's bowling tournaments. I wanted them to be able to come to me when they were hurting and let me wipe their tears and give them hugs. I wanted to be able to talk with them every day-to listen to their laughter, to know their dreams, to say "I love you."

Each time we parted, my heart ached a little more. But on this visit Tracy and Phillip had given me exciting hope for the future. They had talked incessantly about their new computer and how, if I bought one, we would be able to communicate daily!

"Remember, Granny," Tracy squealed as I waved good-bye, "get a computer! And write to us!"

"Every day!" Phillip shouted. "We'll write to you, too."

And so it was that I abandoned my out-dated typewriter and made a frightening leap into this fast-paced, high-tech era of e-mail. Everything about my new computer scared me. I was afraid to touch the keyboard for fear I'd delete something important or do some sort of damage. I even had trouble getting started with the one-page, loose insert of quick tips:

Click on the Windows Icon.

(*Wait!* I wanted to scream. *How do I turn on the computer?*)

Click on the Start button, located on the Taskbar.

(*What's a taskbar?*)

Point to Programs with the mouse cursor.

(*What part of this silly-looking mouse thing is a cursor?*)

Gramps started questioning my sanity when he heard me talking to my machine, aloud, on a regular basis:

WARNING! Invalid MAPI.DLL present. Cannot provide MAPI.DLL service.

(*Did I ask to be serviced?*)

WARNING! This program has performed an illegal operation and will be shut down.

(*So shut down already. I don't want to work with something illegal anyway.*)

WARNING! A printer time-out has occurred.

(What?! My printer is taking a break? Who's in charge here?)

My first few weeks of learning were not fun. I spent full days and nights reading tutorials. I bought Windows for Dummies. I waited on hold for hours, the phone glued to my ear, trying to connect to a live helper on the "helpline." I harassed my friends with annoying calls—at 7:00 A.M., at meal time, at bedtime—pleading for a simple escape from some program jam that had me trapped in limbo.

The machine became my nemesis, and at the same time, the hero that could link me to my family. It was definitely a love/hate relationship. But no obstacle, technological or otherwise, could deter me from the possibility of hearing from my grandchildren every day!

I've missed out on so much of their lives. But with electronic mail, everything has changed. Now, one month and dozens of messages later, I'm up-to-the-minute with news from Tracy and Phillip!

By e-mail, Phillip tells Gramps and me about his role in the school play. He regales us with his account of getting caught in the rain on his bike. And he makes us proud as he announces his test scores in math.

On my last visit I taught him a goofy language called "Op." He recently sent a complete e-mail message using our "secret code"—no easy task. The best part was *OpI lopove yopou sopoopoopoopo mopuch!* Translation: I love you soooo much!

Tracy turned ten last week. We were in on the birthday plans from day one—the porcelain doll she was hoping for, the anticipation of a slumber party with three of her friends and a Lion King cake.

On the night of her sleepover we smiled at the computer message from her dad complaining about the unbearable noise level. We quickly responded to Tracy by saying, "We had to close our windows because we could hear you and your friends all the way across the ocean!"

Her mom immediately replied, "I just went in and read your message to the girls. They started to apologize, then realized it was a joke. The look on their faces was priceless!"

Before long we received a short note from

Tracy. It was almost as though we were right there enjoying her party in person.

The kids write to me when they're happy. And they write when they are hurting. They share some secrets they don't even tell Mom and Dad, and they ask me questions that only a grandma could answer.

I can't wipe their tears or put my arms around them and hold them close. But I can "listen" and show how much I care with my empathy and advice. I can send them funny jokes and precious poems. I can tell them how much I love them—every day.

I still make lots of mistakes on my computer, and my heart still jumps when I get one of those obnoxious, threatening, WARNING! alerts. The most recent one said I had committed a "fatal error." *Fatal!* I nearly threw in the mouse pad! But on the same day we received a message from Tracy saying, "I love you guise bigger than the entire world!"

For *that* I'll take any abuse this whiz-bang wonder of chips and a motherboard dishes out.

Just call me Computer Granny!

Kay Conner Pliszka

A Doll of a Christmas

God does notice us, and he watches over us. But it is through another person that he meets our needs.

Spencer W. Kimball

Often, as adults, we tend to remember the Christmas toys we wanted as children, but never received, and to forget the ones we were given. Later in life we sometimes indulge ourselves with collections of these never-acquired toys. Some women collect teddy bears or delicate music boxes to compensate for the ones they didn't get as little girls, and some men like to collect model cars and train sets to replace the ones they wished for but never found under the Christmas tree.

I suspect that's why, for as long as I can remember, I've collected dolls: big ones, small ones, dolls of all sizes, styles and shapes. And I suppose that's why I display my collection proudly every Christmas season.

Perhaps the events of one Christmas morning, many, many years ago, inspired my devotion and interest in dolls. It all began the year my family moved in with my immigrant grandparents, in their two-story home on the west side of town.

As a little girl growing up in an immigrant household, I experienced a time when money and jobs were scarce for our family, and the only gifts we could afford on holidays and birthdays were an abundance of family love and my grandma's wonderful homemade pasta dinners.

Traditionally, my family celebrated Christmas Eve by attending a solemn midnight mass at the nearby church. It was also traditional to hang one of Grandma's long, black cotton stockings on the mantel every Christmas Eve. Come Christmas morning I would awake to find the stockings filled with fruit and nuts, a generous gift from the "Christmas Angel," or so Grandma told us. Santa Claus had never paid our house a visit; only the Christmas Angel came bearing fruit and nuts.

Coming from a poor, small town in Italy, where it was a struggle to make ends meet, Grandma and Grandpa frowned on the New World's tradition of spending hard-earned money on frivolous gifts. For that reason I stayed indoors on Christmas day, with a faked bellyache, rather than face my new neighborhood friends, who all received bright and shiny new toys on Christmas morning.

However, as time went by, Grandma and Grandpa began to mellow to the modern ideas and rituals of their new country and eventually welcomed the new traditions of Christmas gift-giving.

I can vividly recall that Christmas Eve when Grandma and Grandpa set up their very first Christmas tree. It happened in December of 1945. The family had just welcomed the birth of a new baby. It was a time of great joy and family happiness, prompting Grandpa to gallantly announce that, come that Christmas Eve, for the first time in his home, there would be a decorated Christmas tree and beneath that tree a generous gift for each family member.

That year, my grandpa was working as a store clerk in a busy downtown department store. It was there he'd seen me admiring a lovely hand-woven wicker doll carriage in the store window. The doll carriage was a popular seller that season; every little girl in my neighborhood owned one, except me. I longed to own one of these buggies so that I would fit in with my new modern little girlfriends.

Come Christmas Eve, I was the first to open my gift from Grandpa. I tore eagerly away at the plain brown paper wrapping. A moment later, I was gloriously surprised to discover the beautiful doll carriage I'd seen in the store window. Grandpa, knowing how much I wanted to emulate my new friends, had spent all of his Christmas bonus to buy it for me.

I found it impossible to sleep that night; I was filled with anticipation for Christmas morning. This year, I would have a brand-new gift to share with my friends.

At the first sign of daylight, I ran outside into the front yard, clutching my fine new toy in my hands. I strutted and strolled my carriage like a fine peacock as Grandma and Grandpa watched proudly from the kitchen window. I paraded my doll carriage up and down the sidewalk until, at last, a group of my little friends began to gather inquisitively around my new toy. I stood there, anticipating words of praise and envy, but instead my smiles soon turned to tears.

As Grandpa and Grandma looked on from the window, they heard my little girl-friends cruelly poking fun and laughing at my empty doll carriage. It seems my well-meaning Grandpa had "put the cart before the horse" so to speak, or in this case "the carriage before the doll." He had given me a doll buggy but forgot that I didn't own a doll!

I stood there, humbled before my peers. Humiliated, I dashed back into the house with my empty carriage. Grandpa, who wanted peace at any price, tried to console me by offering to buy me a new doll for my birthday. I appreciated the kind gesture, but my birthday was a month away, and I needed a solution right away. It was Grandma, in her infinite wisdom, who came up with the idea that solved my problem and made that Christmas a day I'd always remember. As far back as I can remember, my extended family has always been there for me, and that day was no exception.

After a few minutes, I reemerged from the house, but this time I was the envy of all the little girls in my neighborhood. Although I didn't have a dolly to call my own, I did have a brand-new baby cousin, who fit snugly into my new doll carriage. Grandma had dressed the new baby in her finest clothes and placed her in my doll buggy, allowing me to take the new infant for an unforgettable stroll around the block.

Fifty years later, I remember that Christmas morning as though it were yesterday. I also remember that one of those little girls offered to trade me her doll for my little baby cousin, and Grandma never knew how close I came to making the trade. It was quite a temptation, but I finally said, "Naw, I'll keep this one. It's got all movable parts!"

Cookie Curci

The Smooth Stone

What the heart knows today the head will understand tomorrow.

James Stephen

When I was a boy I didn't know I loved my grandmother. Being around her was more fun than being around most people, and I thought of her as the center of all good things. She could make taffy that just disappeared in your mouth and sent bright sparks of vanilla playing on your tongue. She could find any herb you might need for a stomach-ache or cough or sore muscles somewhere in the woods near her farm. She could tell a

better story than you might ever hear anywhere else, and she could understand me
when I tried to sort out the confusing parts of
life.

What lasts in recall of her is how she
helped people—including me—put confusion to rest. She didn't lecture or explain how
things ought to be; she just walked along
beside me, and we looked at the world
together.

One summer when I was fourteen and
having a rough time with growing up, I spent
the month of June with her. My parents, I
think, were eager to be rid of me after the
school year. I have no idea now why I fought
with them in the way that I did, but I know
that fighting back seemed important to do. I
wasn't going to let anyone run roughshod
over me even if I knew I was in the wrong
about staying out late, or taking the car on
my own, or going into the city to see a movie.

My grandmother lived in a very small town
in the mountains of Kentucky. Everyone
knew her, and everyone knew me. She did
not drive and had no car so there was no
problem about my driving anywhere, and

there was nowhere in the county to stay out late because most people were farmers and "went to bed with the chickens" as people used to say.

I spent my days working on the land, helping mend fences or hauling rocks, and often in the afternoon my grandmother and I would go walking. I called it "hiking." She said it was "walking" because "hiking" meant you were going someplace.

"Honey," she said to me that day, "we don't know where we're going. We're just out in creation and takin' things in."

We walked for a time along the edge of the woods that bordered her property and led eventually down to a fast-flowing creek that had clear, sweet water even in summer. She walked in an easy deliberate way that gave her time to spot four-leaf clovers or mushrooms. We stopped many, many times to look at something: a snake's dusky burrow or a red-winged blackbird's nest.

There was something on my mind, but I didn't know exactly what it was. After a time, we climbed down the stony bank of the creek and waded in the cool, fast water. I liked to watch it roll over the rocks in the creek bed and the feel of it between my toes.

A fallen trunk of an old maple tree almost spanned the creek at one point, and my grandmother took off her shoes and left them on the bank. Then she waded into the water to the old tree and sat on it so that her feet were in the water up to her ankles.

For some reason or other I began to collect stones. Small egg-shaped stones, gray and white. Stones shaped like little hard cookies and—the prime object of my quest—stones that were almost round. I was very picky about what I chose to keep and often would toss back something I found after I'd examined it closely and found that it came up short of my expectation.

Then I heard myself say, "My dad would never do this."

"Do what, Honey?"

"Sit on a log and watch me hunt stones."

"Oh," she said. And nothing else.

I worked my way down toward the edges of the stream where the best stones often were and continued my hunt in the dappled, leaf-filtered light. The air was warm and smelled faintly of mint. My father was much in my thoughts lately because I had so much trouble with him.

He was a doctor, and it seemed to me he thought he knew everything there was to know. He pushed me pretty hard, I thought. Just then, as I was thinking about him, I reached my hand into the water and out it came holding a perfectly round piece of white quartz. It was round as a marble almost. I splashed through the water to show it to my grandmother.

She took it from me and held it between her thumb and forefinger. She looked at a long time, turning it this way and that in the light.

"Right pretty," she said. "You'll keep this one?"

"Oh, yeah, I sure will. It's perfect. Isn't it?"

"I'd say so," she said. She gave it back to me. Then she said, "Why don't you just pick up rocks from the bank instead of going to all the trouble of searching the water?"

"There aren't any good stones on the bank."

"What do you mean? A stone is a stone."

I looked closely at her to see if she was teasing me and saw that she was very serious.

"No, Grandmother," I said patiently. "The stones on the bank are all rough."

"You like smooth stones?"

"Yes, I do." I held up my newfound treasure and thought again how lucky I'd been to find it.

"You know how they get that way? How they get smooth like you like?"

"The water does it," I said, glad that I knew that.

"Yes. And it does it by rubbing the stones together. Over and over. Years and years. Until all the rough edges are gone. And then the stones are beautiful. Sort of like people."

I looked directly into her eyes—they were almost the color of cornflowers—astonished that I suddenly, somehow knew what she meant.

She rubbed her hand through my hair, messing it up. "Think of your daddy like the water, Honey, and one day when you are a splendid man, you'll understand how you got that way." And that was all she said that day to me about important things. And it was enough.

Walker Meade

Passing the Torch

Pretty much all the honest truth-telling there is in the world is done by children.

Oliver Wendell Holmes

Summer 1964, a northwoods lake.

"Get up! Get up!" my mother whispers.

My eyes flash open. Confusion clouds my brain. Where am I? Is something wrong? I quickly look around.

I'm sandwiched between frayed woolen blankets and the sagging mattress of an old metal bed on the porch of our family log cabin. Looking almost exactly as it did when my grandparents built it in 1929, it sits high on a hill surrounded by the pine and musty fragrance of the woods.

Through sleepy eyelids I take in the dark-green porch swing, the birch leg table, and the smoky glass of the corner kerosene lantern reflecting the stillness of the lake below.

Having escaped the steamy cornland of my home for a few summer weeks, I believe I'm in heaven on Earth. My face feels the coolness of the early morning air. I relax and curl deeper beneath the blankets' warmth.

"Get up!" my mother's voice whispers again. "You must come now. The sunrise is simply glorious!"

The sunrise? Get up to see the sunrise? Who's she kidding? The last thing this fourteen-year-old wants to do is leave a warm bed to go see a sunrise, glorious or otherwise. It's 5:00 A.M. and freezing out there.

"Hurry!" my mother urges.

Being careful not to let the screen door slam, she sets off down the forty-nine long steps at a determined rate of speed to the lake below.

In the twin bed opposite me, my seventeen-year-old sister Nancy stirs. She pushes back the covers and plops to the floor. Not to be outdone, I make a supreme effort and struggle out of bed as well. In our thin cotton nighties, we grab my father's WWII pea-green army blankets from the foot of our beds and wrap them tightly around our shoulders.

As our bare feet touch the cold porch floor, we are thunderbolted awake. Our pace quickens. One of us misses catching the screen door. It slams. Like a couple of water bugs hopscotching across the lake in avoidance of fish jaws, we gingerly pick our way over slippery rocks and prickly pine needles down the forty-nine dew-covered log steps to the lake shore.

When we feel we've saved our feet from any horny toads or big black spiders that might be crazy enough to be up this early, we catch our breath and look up. Our mother's silhouette is outlined against a rosy dawn, the first light catching the soft red of her hair. She is right. It is a glorious sunrise.

Across the lake a sliver of the most brilliant red crests the top of the shadowed forest. Hues of lavender, rose and amber begin to pulsate into the sky like a heavenly kaleidoscope. High above in the soft blueness, a lone star still sparkles. Silver mist rises gently from the smoothness of the lake. All is still. In the sacred silence, my mother, sister and I stand reverently together against a backdrop of tall pine and watch the magic of God's dawning unfold.

Suddenly, the curve of a brilliant sun bursts through the dark forest. The world begins to awake. We watch a blue heron rise up from a distant shore and gently fan its way over still waters. Two ducks make a rippled landing near our dock while the black and white beauty of a loon skims along the edge of a nearby island hunting for its morning food.

Breathing in the chill air, the three of us draw our blankets closer. The soft hues of the sunrise turn into the brightness of a new day and the last of the stars fades. My sister and I take one more look, race up the steps, and jump into our beds to grab a few more hours of sleep.

My mother is more reluctant to leave the

sunrise's amphitheater. From the renewed warmth of my bed, it is a while longer before I hear her reach the top step and gently close the porch door.

Summer 1994, a northwoods lake.

"Get up! Get up!" I whisper to my adolescent sons sleeping dreamily in the same old metal beds of our family's cabin porch.

"Come see the sunrise! It's awesome!"

Amazingly, I watch as this fourth generation of cabin snoozers rouse themselves from cozy comfort. They snatch the WWII pea-green army blankets from the foot of their beds and stumble out the porch door. It slams. Gingerly they maneuver slippery rocks and prickly pine needles down forty-nine dew-covered log steps to the lakeshore.

Their seventy-four-year-old grandmother is already there. Her red hair, now streaked with white, reflects the first light.

She greets her grandsons with the quiet of a bright smile, gathers her blanket closer, and turns toward the east to observe once again God's dawning.

My sons' faces watch intently as the rich colors of the sunrise soar up into the sky like the brilliant plumage of a great bird. It isn't long before the flap of a blue heron's wing or the melodic call of a loon awaken the lake with activity.

"Isn't it beautiful?" I whisper.

The boys nod in silent agreement. Their grandmother smiles at them. Before long, they grab the tails of their frayed blankets and race back up the steps to the welcomed warmth of their beds.

My mother and I stay a little longer. Standing close, we watch the swirls of pearl mist rise and the sky bloom into the shades of a morning rose. We are rewarded this morning by the graceful glide of an eagle high overhead. The gentle rays of the early sun warm our faces.

Eventually, we turn to begin our slow climb up the old log stairs. Halfway up, I catch my breath and look back to see how my mother is doing. But she is not there. She has changed her mind, and through the treetops I can see her, still on the lakeshore, lingering in the light.

Marnie O. Mamminga

Worms and All

Laughter is the lightening rod of play and the public and private sharing of joy.

Source Unknown

I stood in my grandparents' kitchen, watching the steam curl through the air above the big pot on the stove. It was an annual ritual as far back as memory would take me. Grandpa was making jelly.

Unable to stand for long periods of time because of arthritic knees, Grandpa would get his juices cooking, then drag over one of the kitchen chairs and sit next to the stove. With an elbow propped on the countertop, he stirred the big pot with a wooden spoon. I would tiptoe to see what it looked like, but I was too small to peek over the top. From what I could tell, though, Grandpa couldn't stretch high enough to see in, either.

"How can you tell when it's ready, 'Pa?"

"I can tell."

He could smile at my impatient fidgeting. Most children like jelly, but to me, Grandpa's was special. It was made from the plums we picked in the yard. While he picked the ones still swinging high in the branches of the little plum tree, I picked up the ones that had been knocked down. Green, overripe or bruised, my contributions were tossed right along with his into the bucket.

Washing the plums in the sink, Grandpa would sort out and discreetly dispose of the unsuitable fruit. Then we steamed the plums, strained the juices and prepared the jars. Quite possibly I was more of a hindrance than a help, but Grandpa never complained or lost patience.

I can remember the first time he told me his recipe.

"There's an art to making good jelly," he lowered his voice and told me. "Worms an' all, Pammy, that's the secret. Worms an' all."

Aghast, I'm sure I made faces while telling him I'd never eat worms. No way! Grandpa threw back his head and laughed. Amusement danced in his eyes.

Then at long last the jelly was ready to eat. Jelly jars sat in rows on the tabletop, with the sunlight shining through the window behind. The deep maroon color would lighten to a brilliant red, and the gold tops and rims would glow. We spooned jelly onto bread and folded it over into sandwiches.

I watched Grandpa take that first bite. Surely if there were worms involved, he wouldn't be eating it, would he? Feeling assured that it was another of Grandpa's jokes, I began to eat, too.

Grandma eyed us both suspiciously.

"Merle, have you been telling her there were worms in those plums? Mercy! Don't you be listening to him, Girl. He just says that so they'll be more jelly left for him."

Grandpa laughed deeply as he spooned more jelly onto the bread.

Each year was the same. While stirring the juice over the stove, Grandpa would share his recipe with me. He would lower his voice and bend over so he could look me in the eye, telling me, "Worms an' all, Pammy. That's the secret." Then the laughter would come. I imagined that this was a secret he was passing down only to me. Quite possibly, though, he spoke softly just so Grandma wouldn't hear from the next room.

The year after Grandpa passed away, my new husband and I moved into a little home in the country. There was a lovely little wild plum tree in the backyard. I waited eagerly for those tiny hard, green plums to ripen so I could try my hand at jelly-making. It took almost a week of gathering daily to get enough to make even one batch of jelly. I carefully sorted, washed and double-checked the fruit.

Following what I could remember from watching Grandpa all those years ago, I succeeded in making a passable plum jelly at my first attempt. Proud of my accomplishment, I showed the shelf full of jelly jars to my dad.

He held one up and admired the sunlight shining red through the glass. I imagined his taste buds watering for his first bite. Then I mentioned that I had used Grandpa's recipe.

The look of delight faded from Dad's face as he turned slowly to look at me. Then he asked, "Worms and all?"

I nodded.

At the end of his visit, Dad only took one jar home with him. His lack of interest in my culinary skills didn't bother me, though.

As I spread a sweet spoonful onto a bit of toast, I thought with a smile, it just leaves more jelly for me!

Pamela Jenkins

What's a Grandma to Do?

What's so simple even a small child can manipulate it? Grandma.

Janet Lanese

One of the most pressing problems for grandparents these days is knowing how to be a grandparent. I certainly don't wear cotton flowered dresses and big full-sized aprons and bake molasses cookies every week like Grandma Kobbeman did. I don't sit on a porch swing and rock the evening away or watch soap operas like my Grandmother Knapp did. When I was fifty and a grandmother, I water-skied behind my brother's boat in Kentucky and snorkeled for hours in the ocean off the coast of two Hawaiian islands. The next year I rode every scary roller-coaster ride at Disneyland.

Grandparents are different nowadays. We have full-time careers. We run corporations and marathons. We belong to clubs, watch the stock market, eat out a lot, exercise regularly and still have the energy to do the Twist at wedding receptions.

My five grandchildren live out of town, and I don't see them on a daily or weekly basis. In fact, since their parents have busy careers and whirligig lives like I do, I'm lucky if I get to see my grandchildren once or twice a month.

When Hailey was four years old she came for her very first "all alone" visit. She would be alone with me Saturday night, all day Sunday, all day Monday and half of Tuesday before her mother arrived to take her back home. Saturday night and Sunday were a breeze. Hailey, her favorite blankie, latest Beanie Baby and I, snuggled together in my big bed. We slept just fine until Hailey sat up in the middle of the night and whispered, "Gramma, you were snoring."

All day Sunday we kept busy with my daughter-in-law and other granddaughter who were visiting for the day. But on Monday morning when Miss Hailey and I woke up and she assured me that I didn't snore at all that night, I began to fret. *It's Monday, a workday. I have books to read and review and a book proposal to get out. I need to be in my home office! How am I ever going to get it all done if I have to entertain Hailey all day?*

I'll worry about it later, I thought. For at that moment there were little girl hugs to be had, waffles to toast, and birds to feed on the deck with my four-year-old helper.

And so we hugged and rocked and ate, and I held the bird feeder while Miss Hailey scooped up six big cups full of tiny seed into the feeder and only a half-cup or so landed on the deck.

As we sat in the glider swing on the deck watching the squirrels eat the bird feed I began to worry again. *I have a column to write and a talk to prepare.* And yet I wanted to be with Hailey. After all, we only had a day and a half left before her mother came. But my work. I needed to work. Or did I?

"Grammie, can we put up the hammock? We could take a nap in it!"

"Let's go to the shed and find the hammock," I said gleefully. We hung the chains on the hooks in the big trees in the backyard and hopped aboard. As we watched a yellow finch and two cardinals flit around the branches high above us as we lay on our backs in that big double-wide hammock, I knew for certain that I was taking the next day and a half off work. Completely.

Hailey and I drew huge pictures on the driveway, using up a whole bucketful of sidewalk chalk. Then she wanted to climb up into her Uncle Andrew's old tree house. She swept all the leaves off the tree-house floor and only about half of them landed on my head. We took a long bike ride on the bike path near my house. I walked while Hailey rode her tiny two-wheeler with the training wheels.

"Grammie, can we go down by the creek?" Miss Hailey squealed when she saw the water.

"Sure! Maybe we'll catch a frog!"

Later that morning we jumped in the car, went shopping for shoes and found just the perfect pair for my wide-footed grandchild. Then we headed to the playland at McDonald's for lunch. Later that afternoon we ate Combos and candy at the $1.99 movie as we giggled at the funny songs in *Cats Don't Dance.*

"Grammie, are you sure there aren't any rules at your house?"

"I'm sure."

"No bedtime?"

"Nope."

"I can stay up until you go to bed?"

"Yup."

"Until late?"

"Sure. We can sleep late tomorrow. You just sit here in my lap so we can snuggle, and I'll read you a couple of books."

"I love you, Grammie."

And so, that's how I learned the true meaning of the words I have laminated on top of my computer: WRITE THINGS WORTH READING OR DO THINGS WORTH WRITING.

I learned that doing things like spending

an entire day and a half playing with a granddaughter is infinitely more important than sticking to a work routine and getting things done in the office. I learned that grandmothers today often need to abandon their schedules, meetings, clubs, activities, workload and appointments, and sometimes spend hours at a time drawing silly animals on the driveway or staring at the leaves from a hammock with a four-year-old's head snuggled in the crook of your arm.

Patricia Lorenz

She'll Call Me "Ma"

When doubts filled my mind, your comfort gave me renewed hope.

King David

"Guess what—I'm pregnant!" My step-daughter phoned. Her joy was obvious. "That's wonderful," I said. "I'm going to be a grandmother!" We had always been close-bonded together by our mutual love for her father. I was sure that my love for this child was big enough to share with her child. What I wasn't sure of was my grandmother-ing ability.

I had often witnessed these women at

church fellowships—huddled in a circle like football players planning their next play. They all had sweet names like "Mimi," "Nana," "Grammy" and "Grandma." Their purses bulged with photos that could be wielded out at a moment's notice. Their conversations revolved around sippy cups, Big Bird and onesies (which I had already mispronounced at a friend's baby shower as "o-nee-zees"). I, on the other hand, was young (only forty) and inexperienced and the stepgrandmother. I had lots of questions and all the fated answers. Would my step-daughter pull away from me? It would only be natural that she grow closer to her real mother in the coming months. Would I suddenly feel like an outsider when my husband stepped into his role as grandfather? Blood is thicker than water. Would I ever get to be involved in this child's life? Never mind quality time . . . I would take any time. What would I be called by this child? "Stepgrandmother" would definitely not conjure up any warm, fuzzy feelings. And I knew that "Mimi," "Nana," "Grammy" and "Grandma" would quickly be claimed by the two grandmothers, two great-grandmothers and one great-great-grandmother who waited in the wings.

My relationship with my stepdaughter deepened as we talked our way through the months of waiting. "I just found out I'm having a girl," she cried. "You are coming to the baby shower, aren't you?"

"Of course I'll be there . . . if it's okay with your mom," I replied. Silence. Neither one of us needed to be reminded of our situation.

Two months later, it was finally time. "We're leaving for the hospital," her voice quivered. "We're on our way," I said. As my husband and I stepped off the elevator, we were greeted by our blended family. Time seemed to crawl as we all awaited the blessed arrival. Finally, she was here. "I'm a grandma!" I blurted out. All heads snapped to attention in my direction.

Had I said that out loud? I hadn't meant to. I suddenly imagined a sign over the hospital room door: "Only blood relatives admitted." I sheepishly smiled and stepped back as we all entered the room.

She was the most beautiful child (other

than my own) that I had ever laid eyes on! I stood by as each one took his or her turn holding the tiny, red-faced stranger. Flashbulbs popped at every turn. She was so perfect. So tiny. And she possessed an unmistakable feature that drew me to her instantly . . . my husband's loving eyes. I knew I was falling in love with her and longed to cradle her in my arms like the others. Instead, I moved toward the door, trying to stay out of the way. All too soon it was time to go and let Mama and baby rest. My eyes filled with tears. I hadn't gotten to hold her. With all the passing of the baby, I had gotten passed over. Just an oversight during all the confusion, I rationalized. Shouldn't get too attached, anyway. That night, my prayers overflowed with pleas for a true relationship with this child. Opportunity for motherhood well behind me, all I had were memories buried under the difficulties of a bad first marriage. There had never been time for filling in baby books with first steps or first words. My daughter had basically raised herself, while my energy was spent just getting through it all.

I desperately wanted a second chance.

The next day, I woke up anxious to get to the hospital and see my stepdaughter. I secretly hoped that no other relatives would be there so I could have her and the baby all to myself. When we arrived, all was well. Mama and baby rested as my husband and I exchanged labor and delivery stories with our son-in-law. When it came time to go, I felt a lump rise in my throat. I still hadn't held the baby, and I felt silly being that emotional over what seemed like such a small incident. No one could have known how I longed to hold that child. I certainly didn't feel like a stepgrandmother. As far as I was concerned, that was my child and my grandchild in that bed. As I turned to leave, my son-in-law caught my eyes. He saw my emotion and somehow he knew what I had missed the day before. He walked over to the bed, reached in and picked up the baby and handed her directly to me.

More than two years have passed since that day. I now fit in quite nicely with the other grandmothers at church. You see, we have so much in common. I, too, have earned one of these sweet names. Shortly after her first birthday, my granddaughter reached out to me as "Ma." It stuck. Sippy cups now crowd my tea glasses and "o-nee-zees" abide in my lingerie drawer. Big Bird makes a daily appearance in my living room, and a larger-than-life version of Tinky Winky has taken up residence under my bed. And I am always armed and ready for any photo contest that might break out at one of those church fellowships.

I have cradled my granddaughter often and have stored up enough laughs for a lifetime as I have replied to questions like, "Ma, can you come over every day and just paint my fingernails?" I receive more love in a day than I could give back in a lifetime. You see, we have always been close—bonded together by our mutual love for her mother.

As I write this, I am happily awaiting the birth of my second granddaughter and am sure that my love for my first grandchild is big enough to share with her sister. Gone are the doubts. Gone are the questions—she'll call me "Ma."

Jackie Davis

Mrs. Malaprop's Kin

How old would you be if you didn't know how old you were?
Satchel Paige

"Grandma!" yelled four-year-old Cody from my bathroom. "There's a spider in the bathtub! Hurry! Can you fix it?"

Pans clattered as I rushed to get the Thanksgiving turkey ready for the oven. I hadn't wanted to baby-sit this busy morning. But I was drafted. Both parents were working. "Yes, I'll fix it as soon as I can. Don't worry." Grandmas are great fixers. "That faucet is hard to turn, but I can do it and the spider will go right down the drain."

"More Valium," came the worried voice from the bathroom. "I can't hear you."

In a few minutes, I rushed into the bathroom to confront the spider.

"Fixed it!" Cody proudly announced. "Grandma, close your eyes. I don't have my *wonder wear* up yet."

Shutting my eyes, I squinted toward the tub as the last of the yellow stream went down the drain. "You're right, Buddy, that spider is gone."

Firsts are memorable—first bike ride, first evening gown, first kiss, first grandchild. I couldn't wait to become a genuine grandma.

At long last, I got my wish. Cody was born. What an angel. I loved his pink cheeks, bright blue eyes, tousled hair and chubby arms wrapped around a stuffed bear. It was a fact: This was the most adorable grandchild in the world. He was perfect.

When Cody began talking, however, the problem surfaced. He had Mrs. Malaprop's biological genes. You remember Mrs. Malaprop from Richard Sheridan's play, *The*

Rivals. She made verbal blunders an art by replacing words similar in sound with those different in meaning.

His ailment became confirmed. Cody, a daredevil on his tricycle, let out a yell one afternoon. I rushed to open the back door when I heard him fall. He was doubled over.

"It really hurts a guy when he hits his tentacles," he cried.

I hugged him and said the reason for his accident was that his jeans were too large and had slipped down. He agreed. "Maybe I should wear expanders to hold them up."

Further proof of his malapropism came when we went to get my driver's license renewed. "Grandma," he warned me, "make sure your license doesn't perspire. I think you might get unrested."

As his condition advanced, he asked me an important question. "Will Santa's little dorks still make me toys when I'm older?" He paused. "Wait a minute . . . I forgot. The dorks live with Snow White. I mean the other little guys."

Yes, Cody definitely had the affliction, but I hope he has it for a long time. It's wonderful having a grandchild with this enigma. He gives me so many good chuckles.

Since the spider invasion had been resolved, Cody and I went back into the kitchen. I groaned. My giblets had boiled dry and were turning black.

"Don't worry, Grandma," Cody suggested. "We could always get some food at the delicate intestine."

Sharon Landeen

Gramma, Please Don't Make Me Put Them Back!

My granddaughter and I are inseparable. She keeps me wrapped around her little finger.

Gene Perret

When my first granddaughter Lacy was about three or four years old, she was my favorite shopping buddy! I could take her for an afternoon of shopping, and unlike a lot of young children, she never asked for anything.

On one of these shopping outings in early spring, Lacy and I had been in several stores and now we were in a WalMart. As always I had put her in the front of a cart so she could stand and reach all the pretty items. We went up and down several aisles looking at everything. When we got into the children's section, she would reach out, take a dress off the rack and say, "Oh Gramma, isn't this one pretty?" After we both admired it she would hang it back up. This is always how we shopped: We looked, commented, returned the item and moved on. She never asked for these items; she just enjoyed looking at all the pretty things!

We then moved on to the shoe department and as I pushed the cart through the little girls section, she picked up and admired several pairs of shoes. Then she saw a pair of hot-pink (pink being her favorite color), high-top suede boots. Slowly reaching for them, she picked them up and cradled them in her arms. Looking up to me, still holding those boots, she said, "Gramma, please don't make me put them back!"

I was surprised with this sudden pleading and asked, "Miss Lacy, what do you need boots for?" After all it was April, winter was over, and it was almost time to start wearing sandals, not boots.

She replied so sadly, "Gramma, they're huntin' boots!" Trying to conceal my laughter, I asked her, "Exactly why do you need huntin' boots?" I knew this dainty, feminine little girl had never gone hunting with Daddy.

She looked at me with an expression that implied God had given her the dumbest of grammas to raise and she said, "For huntin' Easter eggs!"

I'm not sure how another gramma would have handled this situation. I do know Miss Lacy proudly left that store carrying the sack that held her new hot pink huntin' boots!

Karren E. Key

The Marriage License

I think sometimes a person's spirit is so strong that it never completely leaves the Earth but remains scattered forever among all those who love them.

Chris Crandall

Grandpa was a practical joker. He was a successful businessman, farmer and entrepreneur, but his most memorable trait was his sense of playfulness. He made you want to be around him, and if nothing else, you wanted to see what was going to happen next.

Grandpa Eric, at eighty-seven, needed to

renew his notary license and called upon his friend and partner Terry Parker to drive him to the Sacramento County recorder's office to complete the task. Terry and her father had worked with Eric in the real estate business for years and were well acquainted with his shenanigans. They knew to look for the twinkle in his eye, which was their cue to go along with anything Eric said or did. The payoff for going along with the practical joke was a guarantee of a good belly laugh and a terrific story to tell anyone who came into the office.

Terry and Eric must have been a comical sight together. Eric's mobility was questionable, his sight was undependable, he was sporting a big Stetson hat, two hearing aids and an unlit cigar. Terry supported his arm walking up the steps of the county recorder's office, but it was challenging for the two of them to maneuver through the door. Terry was nine months pregnant with a sixty-inch waist, swollen feet and a bladder reduced by pressure to the size of a small cocktail olive. They just barely made it through the office door only to notice the long, long line up to the records and licenses window. Eric didn't mind waiting because he was already working on how to turn the wait into a little fun.

It was a busy day in the recorder's office and the staff were working as quickly as they could, fielding many questions, some ridiculous, handing out numerous forms and directing people who were completely lost to other offices.

After about a thirty-minute wait, Terry and Eric made it to the front of the line only to be coolly greeted by an exasperated state employee. Sighing impatiently, she asked, "How can I help you?" From her attitude, it was clear that she was thinking that this old man had probably come in with his daughter to get a power-of-attorney form and could have saved everybody a lot of time if they'd just called ahead and picked one up at their local stationery store. In spite of his age, Eric was a very sharp guy and figured out the woman's impression of him at first glance and couldn't resist the chance to have a little fun. He was thinking, *Let the games begin!*

"We're here for a marriage license!" he demanded loudly as he pounded his fist on the counter. "And speed it up! We've been waiting in line for a half an hour and as you can see my bride-to-be here can't stand much longer." The look of total shock (and negative judgment) on the clerk's face as she processed this bit of surprising information could have stopped a speeding locomotive in its tracks. She was so befuddled that she couldn't even muster up enough composure to cover her shock and said, "Why I thought I'd seen everything in my thirty years of working here, but this takes the prize!"

Eric pulled himself up to his full height, puffed his chest out, looked her in the eye and said, "I'm not getting any younger here, so let's not take all day about it." Terry had a decision to make: let this gal off the hook or go along with the joke. She was also doing everything in her power not to burst into laughter at the ridiculous request, not to mention the hilarious look on the clerk's face. She went for it. She put on her best game face, one that resembled a desperate gold-digging bride who'd found her sugar daddy at the eleventh hour of the game. She also looked very uncomfortable—which was not part of the joke, since she was afraid she was going to laugh so hard that her "tears" would run down her legs.

Eric let that poor clerk run all over that office looking for a marriage license. She was so disconcerted that a simple daily task turned into the search for the Lost Ark. The clerk stopped at each secretary's desk, soundlessly whispering to them, shaking her head and pointing to Terry and Eric. Shocked stares and rolled eyes refocused on the odd couple.

At long last the clerk came back with the necessary paperwork and with an incredulous expression asked Eric if he knew that in the state of California he needed blood tests to get married in case of infectious diseases. "I don't know where she's been before I got hooked up with her, but at my age I guess I'm ready to take the leap of faith. What do you think?" An unrecognizable sound came out of the clerk's mouth as she shoved the paperwork in his direction. Eager to go to the ladies' room, Terry was wondering just how long Eric was going to keep the clerk in suspense when suddenly he smiled and said, "Gotcha! We're really here to renew my notary license!"

At this point Terry was sure the practical joke had run its course and dashed to the ladies' room, not a moment too soon. When she returned to collect Eric and his renewed license, the entire office was laughing with him, including the clerk who was a good sport considering the joke was at her expense. After that day, whenever he had any business in the recorder's office he asked for her by name.

Meladee McCarty

The Rodeo Grandmas

The sky is my ceiling and the ground is my carpet.

Judy Golladay

Did you ever read an article in a magazine or newspaper about someone so very interesting that you really wished you could meet them personally? Me, too. That has happened many times, but I thought I'd never have the opportunity to follow through. Recently, however, I read a story about four ladies called, "The Rodeo Grandmas." Dressed in boots, ten-gallon hats, chaps, vests and carrying lariats, they seemed to be the embodiment of all that was and is good about the West. Tough enough to work outdoors on the range, skilled enough to win trick roping contests, tender enough to touch the hearts of so many people—these ladies had a twinkle in their eyes and an openness in their smiles, which came jumping off that magazine's pages and simply got to me. I decided that this was it, the moment to take thought and turn it into action. I ordered an airline ticket to Ellensburg, Washington, and called the Rodeo Grandmas to see if I'd be welcome. "Come on ahead! The ladies will be delighted to meet you!" said their spokesperson, Mollie Morrow, a photographer in their town. Molly picked me up at the airport and treated me to a short history of the group on our ride from Yakima. Even with her thorough introduction, I was not quite prepared to meet these unusual ladies.

Molly took me to her studio where I met Lorraine, Janis, Chloe and Peggy. Sitting around the small studio were the smilingest, most welcoming group I've met in a very long time. The Rodeo Grandmas, from sixty-five to eighty-nine, had been selected by an

advertising agency that was designing a
new series of ads for the Washington
Mutual Bank in 1993. The agency had
wanted a series of unusual people to high-
light—trying to make the connection that
their bank was "something different" from
the ordinary. They'd put out a call for
grandmas—grandmas who could ride and
rope and even compete in rodeos. Nearly
thirty women from this area had shown up
and, within a few hours, the producers had
unerringly selected four women who seemed
to embody a special spirit—independence,
high energy, high skills and toughness mixed
with tenderness.

They shot their commercial and left. It
was a one-shot deal. Washington Mutual's
series would show many other kinds of special, unusual people. But when it aired, the
reaction was dramatic: Everyone wanted to
see more of those "rodeo grandmas"!

The agency came back and shot more
commercials. And, bit by bit, the Rodeo
Grandmas became a tight-knit group. The
producers had chosen well. Somehow they
clicked as a group. One of their number,

Judy Golladay, had revealed to the group, and to the producers, that she'd just been diagnosed with breast cancer. Despite that, they all agreed she'd continue as a part of the group. She was having radiation and chemotherapy even as the commercials were being shot. For five months out of every year, she had lived out on the range, with just her horse and dog as company. She was simply a cowgirl, in touch with the earth as few modern Americans are anymore. She spoke of the sky as her ceiling and the ground as her carpeting. Perhaps that sounds corny to someone citified, but Judy meant it and lived it. When the going got tough, she'd climb up on her horse and head out for the hills with her dog and soak in the peacefulness she found in that environment.

There was good news: The treatments had worked! Judy's cancer went into remission. And the Rodeo Grandmas began a series of appearances all over the northwest. Wherever Washington Mutual needed them to appear, they'd show up in full regalia, riding in on horseback, roping and hollering,

"Yippie-ty-yi!" and "Howdy, Buckaroos!" They enjoyed playing with the stereotypes and making them real. Pretty soon they began receiving invitations to lead the opening parade at rodeos or to appear at shopping malls and hospitals and retirement homes.

What a deep chord they struck in western hearts! As they'd ride into the arena leading the parade, you could hear the crowd noise change: A dull roar became louder, more focused, more joyous. You could track their location by the change in the sound from the audience: "They're here, the Rodeo Grandmas!" Cheers rose spontaneously, children waved, everyone was excited. Little kids came up to them demanding (and getting) hugs.

Once, on the way to the airport for yet another appearance in another city, there was a major traffic jam. All cars were stopped. The grandmas were sitting quietly in their van waiting for the jam to clear. Suddenly, the occupants in a nearby car spotted them. There was a tap at the window of their van. "Are you the Rodeo

Grandmas?" the driver of another car, standing in the road, asked. "IT'S THE RODEO GRANDMAS!!!" he shouted to all the other cars. "IT'S REALLY THEM!" And there, in the roadway, cars stopped bumper-to-bumper, and a crowd formed, cheering for them and requesting autographs.

At their appearances, children line up to learn roping—throwing their lariats at a practice steer and lighting up with joy when they make it. And there, over at the end of the line of Rodeo Grandmas, is Lorraine, sitting comfortably, with a line of kids waiting to be taught how to yodel.

"Something about being a grandma and being up on a horse seems to be the attraction," said Peggy, seventy-four, an accomplished trick roper. "They just think that someone on a horse has to be honest." At twenty she was a Rodeo Princess and met a famous trick rider, Monte Montana, who took a liking to her and sent her a gift of a trick-riding saddle. Her rodeo career took off. But life has a way of interrupting one's plans, and she got married, became a secretary and raised four children. "I used to do the Cossack Drag," she told me. "Some people call it the Suicide Drag, but I'm not doing trick riding now. I also used to spin four ropes at once. One I held in my mouth, one on my foot and one in each hand. Today I just do three. You've got to know what you're capable of," she confided.

Janis, at sixty-five, does team roping with a partner, catching steers in competition. In fact, she competes in events with her grandson! "When I was born, my dad sold a horse off for eighty dollars to pay the hospital bill. That was a lot of money then. So horses have always been in my blood. My dad didn't have any sons, so my sister and I became the boys of the family." Then she added an afterthought, as though I might think her too much the tomboy, "We can be real ladylike, too, you know." I nodded my agreement. "My dad called me, 'Toughie,' and he taught me how to ride. I've learned to draw strength from my horses. You have a relationship with your horse, you see, and if you've got tears to shed, your horse will listen and be there for you. It's hard to explain to anyone who hasn't had this experience, but it's really true." All the ladies agreed.

Chloe said, "I've heard it said that 'the best thing for the insides of a man is the outside of a horse.' The relationship with your horses is almost therapeutic. In fact, when Judy's cancer returned and she knew how bad it was, she saddled up and took her horse and dog up into the hills for one more time. She spent some weeks up there and it gave her a lot of peace."

Chloe replaced Judy in the group. "I was kind of the wrangler—Lorraine's my mom, and I was going to all the Rodeo Grandmas' events anyway, so they kind of corralled me into it. And I love being in the Rodeo Grandmas with my mom." She patted Lorraine's knee. "Kinda amazing, huh? Sometimes when we're at a show, and we get set up to teach roping and stuff, the kids come running at us in waves and surround us. It's an incredible feeling to see that, and they all seem to want to touch my mom." Lorraine grins at me.

Lorraine met her husband at a stock show in 1928 and is now not only a grandmother of eleven, she's a great-grandmother of nineteen. Her horse is a little too spirited for her now, but she does ride occasionally. Still, she is ready to teach you how to yodel and will give you a hug at the drop of a ten-gallon hat.

The Rodeo Grandmas are not media people, although they've been affected by their media appearances. They've retained their hometown values and style, despite being on *Entertainment Tonight*, *The Rosie O'Donnell Show*, and on countless radio and TV interviews.

You get a clear message from being with these ladies that they don't sit around fretting about "the meaning of life." Instead, they take action, and they know that life is meaningful. As Lorraine says, "We only did what had to be done. There's nothing special in that. You do the tasks the Lord puts in front of you."

Peggy added, "You have to have something to get up for in the morning." It was clearly the secret of these gals' healthiness and continued strength, that their lives had given them purpose and continue to do so. Chloe smiled and said, "I've learned to put my heart into what I'm doing." Her mom looked at her proudly, smiling, too. Janis continued, "When you sit in the rocking chair, you just don't get anywhere."

"I think I was born to be a Rodeo Grandma," Peggy declared, looking serious. "Everything in my life seemed to be aimed in this direction. I knew there was something special going to be in my life, and look, here it is!" And she tells me that none of the Rodeo Grandmas has ever broken more than a finger or a toe and that Lorraine has never spent the night in a hospital. "Builds your muscles, expands your chest, makes you breathe more deeply—and that's just when you get on the horse. Go riding a bit and you'll really get some exercise. It's a good, clean life."

It was the end of a glorious day, spent in the company of these tough and tender ladies, and I really didn't want to leave. Each one hugged me, and I readily hugged back. "Lorraine," I said, choking up a bit, "I've just about run out of grandmas in my life. I wonder if you'd be my grandma?"

She beamed at me and gave me an extra

squeeze, "Why sure, honey, you can be my little buckaroo!"

On the trip back home I was still filled with the experience of being with them and pondered what I'd learned, or maybe relearned. It was clear that they'd lived a lifestyle that was healthy and unambiguous. What had to be done had to be done, no two ways about it. They had built fun and humor into every day whenever possible. They had been the kind of people you can count on—and there's something powerfully reassuring in being around people like that. They'd not retired from life but were still actively engaged in it, every day. Connecting with people and making a difference in their lives have kept them going, too. Although their lives had most of the same elements in them before, each had been profoundly changed by becoming a Rodeo Grandma. It enabled them to see themselves on a wider stage, and gave them an opportunity to be a model for others, whether they were kids or grandparents. How to live a life with integrity, how to organize yourself so that the important things got done—these were not inconsequential things. But they don't preach these concepts; they simply live them day by day.

I wasn't kidding when I asked Lorraine to be my grandma, for my own are long gone, and there's something missing in my life, too: someone older and wiser, someone who also knows when it's time to give a hug or share a grin. I'm making plans to go visit Grandma Lorraine, and, who knows, she just might teach me to yodel!

Hanoch McCarty

More Chicken Soup?

We enjoy hearing your reactions to the stories in *Chicken Soup for the Soul* books. Please let us know what your favorite stories were and how they affected you.

Many of the stories and poems you enjoy in *Chicken Soup for the Soul* books are submitted by readers like you who had read earlier *Chicken Soup for the Soul* selections.

We invite you to contribute a story to one of these future volumes.

Stories may be up to 1,200 words and must uplift or inspire. To obtain a copy of our submission guidelines and a listing of upcoming *Chicken Soup* books, please write, fax or check our Web sites.

Chicken Soup for the Soul
P.O. Box 30880
Santa Barbara, CA 93130
fax: 805-563-2945
Web site: *www.chickensoup.com*

Supporting Grandparents

The busyness of daily life and the physical distances between families make it more difficult for grandparents to play the powerful role they have traditionally played in the lives of their grandchildren. A portion of the proceeds from sales of the book, *Chicken Soup for the Grandparent's Soul* is donated to support a wonderful program that helps directly with these issues.

The Foundation for Grandparenting is a not-for-profit, tax-exempt corporation. Since 1980, they have been dedicated to raising grandparent consciousness and grandparent identity. Through education, research, programs, communication and networking, they promote the benefits of grandparenting, and the involvement of grandparents as agents of positive change for their families and society.

One of the most positive programs we've seen is The Foundation's Grandparent-Grandchild Summer Camp, which has helped both local and "long-distance grandparents" to become closer to their grandchildren.

To find out how you can be a part of this program or how you can contribute to it, write to:

The Foundation for Grandparenting
108 Farnham Road
Ojai, CA 93023
Web site: *www.grandparenting.org*

Who Is Jack Canfield?

Jack Canfield is one of America's leading experts in the development of human potential and personal effectiveness. He is both a dynamic, entertaining speaker and a highly sought-after trainer. Jack has a wonderful ability to inform and inspire audiences toward increased levels of self-esteem and peak performance.

In addition to the *Chicken Soup for the Soul* series, Jack has coauthored numerous books, including his most recent release, *The Success Principles, How to Get From Where You Are to Where You Want to Be* with Janet Switzer, *The Aladdin Factor* with Mark Victor Hansen, *100 Ways to Build Self-Concept in the Classroom* with Harold C. Wells, *Heart at Work* with Jacqueline Miller and *The Power of Focus* with Les Hewitt and Mark Victor Hansen.

Jack is regularly seen on television shows such as *Good Morning America, 20/20* and *NBC Nightly News.* For further information about Jack's books, tapes and training programs, or to schedule him for a presentation, please contact:

Self-Esteem Seminars
P.O. Box 30880
Santa Barbara, CA 93130
phone: 805-563-2935 • fax: 805-563-2945
Web site: *www.chickensoup.com*

Who Is Mark Victor Hansen?

In the area of human potential, no one is better known and more respected than Mark Victor Hansen. For more than thirty years, Mark has focused solely on helping people from all walks of life reshape their personal vision of what's possible. .

He is a sought-after keynote speaker, best-selling author and marketing maven. Mark is a prolific writer with many bestselling books such as *The One Minute Millionaire*, *The Power of Focus*, *The Aladdin Factor* and *Dare to Win*, in addition to the *Chicken Soup for the Soul* series.

Mark has appeared on *Oprah*, CNN and *The Today Show*, and has been featured in *Time*, *U.S. News & World Report*, *USA Today*, *New York Times* and *Entrepreneur* and countless radio and newspaper interviews.

As a passionate philanthropist and humanitarian, he has been the recipient of numerous awards that honor his entrepreneurial spirit, philanthropic heart and business acumen for his extraordinary life achievements, which stand as a powerful example that the free enterprise system still offers opportunity to all.

Mark Victor Hansen & Associates, Inc.
P.O. Box 7665
Newport Beach, CA 92658
phone: 949-764-2640 • fax: 949-722-6912
Web Site: *www.markvictorhansen.com*

Who Are Meladee and Hanoch McCarty?

Hanoch and Meladee McCarty have traveled all over the world together working with educators and business professionals on the goal of bringing more kindness and altruism into the world, workplace, home, community and classroom.

Hanoch is an educator and motivator well-known for his high energy and the drama and humor of his presentations. He speaks to school systems, governmental agencies, conventions, college faculties, professional associations, medical practices, health maintenance organizations, dental groups, hospital staffs, law practices and industry groups.

Hanoch is the author and coauthor of over twenty books and training programs to promote his lifelong commitment to the improvement of instruction on all levels.

Meladee is a professional educator and dynamic speaker in the field of special education, working to provide inclusional education settings for children with disabilities. She presents trainings to educators and has extensive experience helping schools and other institutions meet the needs of disabled students and workers. Meladee is a master at using appropriate humor to defuse tension and conflict.

Meladee and Hanoch have a wonderful time working and playing together. They are proud parents and grandparents and committed to bringing more humor and kindness into the world, creating a positive impact on those with whom they come in contact.

To contact the McCartys, write or call:

P.O. Box 66
Galt, CA 95632-0066
phone: 209-745-2212
fax: 209-745-2252
e-mail: *hanoch@bestspeaker.com*

*Each of us leaves a thumbprint
on the world, a record that we
were here and who we were
and what we did. Your only
choice is what kind of
thumbprint to leave.*

Sidney B. Simon

Contributors

If you would like to contact any of the contributors for information about their writing or would like to invite them to speak in your community, look for their contact information included in their biography.

Cookie Curci was born in San Jose, California, and has lived there for fifty-nine years. Her grandparents came to San Jose from Italy at the turn of the century. Their family stories inspired her to write a "Remember When" column for her local newspaper, The Willow Glen Resident, which she has been writing for twelve years. Her family is close-knit, not only emotionally, but also geographically. She considers herself blessed to be living in a community so rich in family heritage.

Jackie Davis resides in Weatherford, Texas, with her husband. She is the mother of one, stepmother of two and stepgrandmother of two. She is a member of North Side Baptist Church where she serves as Coordinator of the Ladies Ministry, and writes and publishes the Ministry's quarterly newsletter.

Pamela Jenkins lives in Henryetta, Oklahoma, where she works as an office manager for Stanley, her veterinarian husband. Her stories have appeared in numerous inspirational publications and on the Internet. She is a member of the Church of Christ, and can be reached by e-mail at *ramblinrabbit@juno.com*.

Karren E. Key is fifty-two years of age and has a blended family of five children and thirteen beautiful grandchildren. Her husband Lacy's job moves them all over the United States, so they rarely are able to live near any of their family. She is making her special memories of each of them even more special.

Sharon Landeen, a retired elementary-school teacher, is the author and illustrator of two bilingual picture books, *When You Get Really Mad* and *Really, Riley!* She enjoys working with youth, was involved for twenty years with 4-H, and is back in the 4-H program with her grandsons. She's a volunteer teacher in reading and art, but still finds time to be "grandmother superior." She can be reached at 6990 E. Calle Arandas, Tucson, AZ 85750 or at *SLLandeen@aol.com*.

Patricia Lorenz is the proud grandmother of Hailey, Hannah, Zachary, Casey and Riley. She's also a full-time writer and speaker who has been published in numerous *Chicken Soup for the Soul* books (*2nd Helping, 3rd Serving, 4th Course, 6th Bowl, Woman's Soul, Single's Soul, Unsinkable Soul, Christian Family Soul,* and *Writer's Soul*). For speaking engagements contact Patricia through Associated Speakers, Inc. at 800-437-7577 e-mail Patricia at *patricialorenz@juno.com*.

Marnie O. Mamminga is a freelance writer and teacher in Batavia, Illinois. Her essays have been published in the *Chicago Tribune, Reader's Digest, The Christian Science Monitor, Lake Superior Magazine* and *Chicken Soup for the Mother's Soul 2*. She has also been a speaker on essay writing at the University of Wisconsin's Writers Institute and the Northern Illinois School Press Association. She received her bachelors and masters degrees from the University of Illinois at Urbana-Champaign. She can be reached at *Mamminga@aol.com*.

Walker Meade began to write stories at the age of fourteen. When he was twenty-two, one of his pieces was published in *Colliers* magazine. He then wrote short fiction for the *Saturday*

Evening Post, *Good Housekeeping* and *Gentleman's Quarterly*, among others. He then turned to writing nonfiction for magazines such as *Cosmopolitan*, *Reader's Digest* and *Redbook*. Later he became the managing editor of *Cosmopolitan* and then the managing editor of *Reader's Digest Condensed Book Club*. His last position in publishing was as president and editor-in-chief of Avon Books. Today he is retired and concentrating on writing longer fiction. Upstart Press published his first novel in August 2001. It has had exciting critical reception and is selling unusually well. The book, *Unspeakable Acts*, can be ordered from *www.amazon.com*.

Kay Conner Pliszka, a retired high-school teacher, motivational speaker and author of humorous and inspirational stories. Her grandchildren bring love and laughter to her life, and compassion and joy to her writing. Kay may be reached at *kpliszka@prodigy.net*.

Harriet May Savitz is the author of twenty books. They include: *Run, Don't Walk*, an ABC Afterschool Special produced by Henry Winkler, *The Lionhearted*, and *On the Move*, reissued by *iuniverse.com*. Also available is *Growing Up at 62: A Celebration*, a book of essays. She can be reached at 732-775-5628.

More great books

#1 New York Times
BESTSELLING AUTHORS
Jack Canfield
Mark Victor Hansen
Paul J. Meyer
Barbara Russell Chesser
Amy Seeger

Chicken Soup for the Golden Soul

Heartwarming Stories About
People 60 and Over

Code #7257 • $12.95

Chicken Soup for the Grandma's Soul

Stories to Honor
and Celebrate the
Ageless Love
of Grandmothers

Jack Canfield, Mark Victor Hansen
and LeAnn Thieman

Code #3285 • $12.95

Also Available

Chicken Soup African American Soul
Chicken Soup Body and Soul
Chicken Soup Bride's Soul
Chicken Soup Caregiver's Soul
Chicken Soup Cat and Dog Lover's Soul
Chicken Soup Christian Family Soul
Chicken Soup Christian Soul
Chicken Soup College Soul
Chicken Soup Country Soul
Chicken Soup Couple's Soul
Chicken Soup Expectant Mother's Soul
Chicken Soup Father's Soul
Chicken Soup Fisherman's Soul
Chicken Soup Girlfriend's Soul
Chicken Soup Golden Soul
Chicken Soup Golfer's Soul, Vol. I, II
Chicken Soup Horse Lover's Soul
Chicken Soup Inspire a Woman's Soul
Chicken Soup Kid's Soul
Chicken Soup Mother's Soul, Vol. I, II
Chicken Soup Nature Lover's Soul
Chicken Soup Parent's Soul
Chicken Soup Pet Lover's Soul
Chicken Soup Preteen Soul, Vol. I, II
Chicken Soup Single's Soul
Chicken Soup Soul, Vol. I-VI
Chicken Soup at Work
Chicken Soup Sports Fan's Soul
Chicken Soup Teenage Soul, Vol. I-IV
Chicken Soup Woman's Soul, Vol. I-II